The Power of Prayer

Believing for a Transformed Life

Melinda Jones Sutton

Copyright © 2023 Melinda Jones Sutton

All rights reserved.

ISBN: 9798859925483

DEDICATION

I dedicate this book back to Jesus Christ for giving me the insight and wisdom to write this prayer journal. To my beloved husband, Chief Apostle Jesse S. Sutton, who I love, honor and cherish for always being a pusher for God's will to be done in my life. To my beloved daughters Shana and Tiffany who have pushed me all the way with encouragement, love and laughter. To the greatest church family on earth: Divine Glory Ministries, Inc. for believing and supporting me.

To all the amazing people who will read this book, may your lives be transformed to live out your divine purpose.

-Melinda Jones Sutton

> "A man cannot move forward while looking back. He's bound to miss opportunities for success. Look ahead."

TESTIMONIAL

"The Power of Prayer (POP) serves as a catalyst that protrudes from the heart of God. THIS prayer book is incomparable to any type of written work done previously. It has had, and continues to make, a global impact. It is changing the lives of God's people, while bringing hope to the hopeless. POP restores the vision of the true power that is found when prayer is activated.

—God's blessings to you, Apostle Melinda Jones Sutton, my beautiful wife, kingdom partner, and God's divine powerhouse."

-Chief Apostle J. S. Sutton

"POP has helped me come into my God given identity that can't ever be manipulated or dictated by people or things." -S. Morris

"I am extremely thankful to God for the Power of Prayer. My life has been changed because I no longer see myself in a negative way, I now know that my validation is in Jesus Christ." -N. Salmon

"As I read POP, it changed my way of thinking and doing. In accepting the word and message of God, I no longer received no other identity outside of God and whom I am."
-Pastor S. Jones

"The Power of Prayer sentenced me to a life of instant, constant and perpetual relationship with my Heavenly Father. The simple truths so skillfully written in this book are constant reminders of who I have always been; God's created masterpiece made in His image and likeness."
-Dr. G. K. Jones

	From My Heart	
	Introduction to the Journey	1
Day 1	Who Am I? Dare to Believe	5
Day 2	Think David & Goliath	8
Day 3	Position Yourself Joshua	11
Day 4	Be Aware of Cain	13
Day 5	Embrace Your Process to Greater: I Am Joseph	16
Day 6	Remove Me from Every Comfortable Place to An Exceptional Place	19
Day 7	I Am Who God Says I Am – I Will accept Nothing Less Than GREATER	22
Day 8	I Am the Servant of the Most High God	25
Day 9	An Untested Faith Will Never Excel You	28
Day 10	No More Training Wheels	31
Day 11	The Rain Must Fall	34
Day 12	God Loves Me and I Accept His Forgiveness Over My Life	37
Day 13	Purpose is My Purpose	40
Day 14	I Will Never Be the Same	43

FROM MY HEART

In August 2015, while at work praying silently, and staring out the window, I remember these exact words, "I am faithful". God has been faithful countless times in my life and in the lives of many. His undeniable love and kindness can't be measured merely by those prayers that He has answered. "Oh no", it can be seen daily through each of us when we show His love towards others. He cares for everyone, and through you and I, we shall be a lifeline for all that need His love.

Answered prayers are God's tools. When tools are used for a specific reason, they accomplish a task. What will one obtain through prayer? One obtains power when the word is being displayed through the lives of others. Open your heart to God for He longs for an opportunity to draw closer to you. We can approach God's throne of grace with freedom and faith. I believe Jesus Christ is calling you into a deeper relationship with Him. I am excited for you, and challenging you, for a renewed life, of trusting a faithful God. Together, we will journey through our past, to experience freedom by casting our cares upon Him, the only one who absolutely cares for us.

God left an advocate, the Holy Spirit, not merely as a reminder, guide, or a comforter. He left Him as a demonstration of His love for us. **John 14:15-18 NIV** *"If you love me, keep my commands. And I will ask the Father, and he will give you another advocate to help you and be with you forever— the Spirit of truth. The world cannot accept him, because it neither sees him nor knows him. But you know him, for he lives with you and will be in you. I will not leave you as orphans; I will come to you."*

The hoped outcome for this prayer journal is in the above passage of scripture—that you become open to God's love and embrace the Holy Spirit as your advocate and guide. Your purpose has been delayed long enough. **John 14:15-18** echoes a vivid picture of His love, and His care. Embark upon this journey of freedom alongside me, leaving behind misplaced trust, and self-preservation, that overshadows the truth of God.

Each title in this journal represents a story of God's faithfulness and the opportunity to examine our character. In this, keep in mind the years you have spent guiding and guarding yourself. Don't allow conviction to overshadow the promise of being free, experiencing God's love, and a new relationship with the Holy Spirit. Every known emotion may surface, every disappointment and unanswered prayer. Nonetheless, allow it to face God's truth concerning you and your destiny.

There is no greater privilege than open access with your heavenly Father. Prayer is a dialogue. As communication takes place, embrace the wisdom you shall receive. This journal will challenge you and incite the Christian you were created to be. As you read and pray, choose a time and place that you are uninterrupted. As with any new journey, there will be interferences, unexpected circumstances, and anxieties. Nonetheless, you aren't here to prove you can succeed. On the contrary, let go, and allow your sovereign God to orchestrate His plans. I can, I shall, and I will agree with my purpose through prayer, and my identity in Jesus Christ. This is your divine opportunity to embrace whom you have been created to be and enjoy becoming that person.

Over the next 14 days, you will experience challenges, you will be encouraged to move forward and to let go. This journey is a reflection of God's redeeming love and His call for reconciliation for you. Use this time to seek His will for your life. God loves you and gives open access to freely communicate with Him. That access is through the Holy Spirit. Will you become receptive to His guidance, His instructions, and accept the truth concerning your life in view of what He will reveal to you? Utilize the blank pages to rewrite your destiny. Freedom awaits you, a successful life, one that is free from every assault against your mind, heart and soul to live a purposeful life in Jesus Christ.

- Melinda Jones Sutton

INTRODUCTION TO YOUR JOURNEY

Many believers are unaware of the power of prayer and the crucial role it plays in the life of the believer, the lives of others, and the bearing it has against the demonic realm. Prayer was established to receive life-changing instruction from our Heavenly Father; it also gives us the ability to confide in our Father. He loves you and I and what parent wouldn't want to give their child "open access"? Yes, He does.

> ➢ ***Let's have effective directional prayers.***
> ➢ ***Let's break haphazard or sound good prayers.***
> ➢ ***Let's bombard heaven with declarations according to scripture.***
> ➢ ***Embrace the Holy Spirit's guide and allow Him access for success.***

- The leading of the Holy Spirit in prayer is a must. The Holy Spirit is not delayed; He will lead you into the realm you are needed, if you allow Him to lead.... **John 14:26 NIV** *"But the Advocate, the Holy Spirit, whom the Father will send in my name, will teach you all things and will remind you of everything I have said to you."*
- The sound or volume of your prayer does not define effective praying.
- One should always incorporate declarations in your prayers.

A. *Intentional, directive prayers are geared towards a specific need.*

Example: If the need is for the widows of our community, the prayer will be guided in every area by the leading of the Holy Spirit to meet the need, to revoke danger, to open hearts to feed, to revise decisions for the widows, to clothe the widows, to send help to meet transportation needs, etc.

Haphazard prayers are those prayers that are intended for a specific need, without being led by the Holy Spirit to intercede for that need. Haphazard prayers are governed by emotions and sound.

- The way to break haphazard prayers is the willingness to be led by the Holy Spirit and to receive instructions for why you are praying. No one knows it all and every believer should be able to listen, receive, learn and be willing to follow the leading of the Holy Spirit.

Let's discuss the purpose to decree, why a believer should implement it during prayer and establish the scriptures as the foundation of prayer through the Holy Spirit.

The Biblical meaning of Decree: is defined as a rule of law issued by a head of state (i.e. President) according to a certain procedure. It has the force of the law. In biblical times, the King had the authority to make decrees. The decree was a very specific written document that was clear about that subject matter. It was law and had to be carried out according to the King's wishes and failure to obey the decree was punishable.

Give God's word an opportunity to be established in your life. When you decree a rule in your life, it's the law; God is our King and His Word should be established as our law.

When I have prayed out of hurt and emotions, I really didn't have any sense of comfort, just times of tears and a feeling of "Will God grant my petitions?". My prayer life changed when I began to implement the scriptures and embrace the Holy Spirit as my guide. My mindset about prayer changed, my heart towards God changed, and I began to experience the joy of praying and the peace of trusting God. I gained confidence, thereby verbally declaring the scriptures in my prayers and not my hurt, pain or emotions. I am free to pray to God and to know He hears me.

Job 22:28 NIV *"What you decide on will be done, and light will shine on your ways."* We have often heard and read this passage of scripture, but have you meditated on the meaning of this powerful word?

There are always conditions that you must meet in order to have the authority to do anything in the Kingdom of God including prayer.

Deuteronomy 28:1 NIV *"If you fully obey the Lord your God and carefully follow all his commands I give you today, the Lord your God will set you high above all the nations on earth."*: When you hear, receive and obey the word of God you are given the power to decree the word.

Psalms 66:18-20 NIV *"If I had cherished sin in my heart, the Lord will not have listened; but God has surely listened and has heard my prayer. Praise be to God, who has not rejected my prayer or withheld his love for me!"*

Holy Spirit: In *John 16:7 NIV* Jesus refers to the Spirit as a "Counselor". One way he'll guide us is by convicting us of sin. And this is really a good thing. God wants us to get rid of the things that displease him, and the only way to identify those things is to be convicted by the Spirit. The Spirit works through our conscience, to make us aware of sin in our lives. The Holy Spirit can help live a life pleasing to God absent of sin.

Romans 8:26 NIV also tells us the Holy Spirit helps us and actually intercedes for us.

Father, I pray for understanding, wisdom and clarity for your divine will to be accomplished in my life. Father, cleanse me of my sins and prepare my heart to pray in a way that will please you. Father, I pray for a true sense of freedom during prayer and an overwhelming joy of knowing the purpose of prayer was accomplished according to your will. Father, draw me closer for a personal relationship with you. Amen.

DAY 1

Who Am I? -Dare to Believe

Ephesians 2:10 NIV *"For we are God's handiwork, created in Christ Jesus to do good works, which God prepared in advance for us to do."*
Lean into His Presence and let God's strength bring you to a place where you can let go of your imagined dreams, desires, fears, hurts, pains, disappointments, cares, concerns, etc. Cry out from that place of loneliness, that place of your pain, that secret hurt of wanting what God offers while wondering, "Does God really know what's best for me to become?". ***1 John 5:14-15 NIV***

Day one of your prayer journey: is the difficult place, the trying place, the testing place. This place requires you to examine who you truly are. **Hebrews 4:6-7 NIV** Stand before a mirror and examine who you see. For most of us, our initial response is to change our outer appearance to satisfy our desire to please others. Today, let's look deeper.

This is the place to challenge your belief system, your relationships, and your life.

Life changing prayers begin when I know who I am, when I know who I've been called to become and when I'm willing to live out that plan.

A realistic believer is never trial free. However, he will identify those challenges in his life that arise to alter or hinder his destiny and be willing to face those challenges without allowing them to shift him from his purpose. **Fill in the blanks and allow transparency.**

Deal with you.

Let it go.

Believe.

Cry out.

Face your future.

~There is hope, give it an opportunity~

Believing in yourself is not impossible.

DAY 2

Think David & Goliath

This is the day after dealing with who you are as well as who you are not. This is the day where you take off all burdens. Burdens that were placed upon you from your childhood. Burdens from those who have given you advice that caused you to spin out of control. Burdens from a relationship that pressed your inner hurt to the surface. Let your "now" face your divine destiny.

Remove the heavy armor that will benefit your now but will destroy your future. Your victory comes through your willingness to let go and embrace God's will for your life. Remove everything. Embrace the endeavors that God has placed before you to achieve. Through His guidance, He will give you strategic approaches, extraordinary talents, and limitless supplies to achieve victory.

David, with what has God entrusted you? Yes, today you are David, and tomorrow, you will arise without hesitations, without regrets, and free from blaming others for seemly misguided instructions.

1 Samuel 17:33-40 NIV *"Saul replied, "You are not able to go out against this Philistine and fight him; you are only a young man, and he has been a warrior from his youth." But David said to Saul, "your servant has been keeping his father's sheep. When a lion or a bear came and carried off the sheep from the flock, I went after it, struck it and rescued the sheep from its mouth. When it turned on me, I seized it by its hair, struck it and killed it. Your servant has killed both the lion and the bear; this uncircumcised Philistine will be like one of them, because he has defied the armies of the living God. The Lord who rescued me from the paw of the lion and the paw of the bear will rescue me from the hand of this Philistine." Saul said to David, "go, and the Lord be with you." Then Saul* *dressed David in his own tunic. He put a coat of armor on him and a bronze helmet on his head. David fastened on his sword over the tunic and tried walking around, because he was not used to them. "I cannot go in these," he said to Saul, "because I am not used to them." So he took them off. Then he took his staff in his hand, chose five smooth stones from the stream, put them in the pouch of his shepherd's bag and, with his sling in his hand, approached the Philistine."*

Father, I release everything in my life that comes to weigh me down. God, I know you are a healer and a deliverer of my soul. You are my Lord and my King, I decree and declare into my life that the cares, concerns, stigmas, strongholds, be it generational or interpersonal, are far from my "now" for forward movement into my purpose. Father, I speak purity of my heart and mind. I decree and declare that my emotions, my will are in line with your word over my life. Abolish and eradicate all attachments that were spoken into my life, forced upon me, and those things I opened doors to obstruct my success. Father, in the name of Jesus, I embrace your plan, your purpose, and I embrace the reason why I was created. I decree and declare that everything that happened against me or to me shall be my catalyst to "greater". I will no longer weep over my experiences. God I decree and declare they are my steppingstones for greater glory, greater victory, and greater abundance in life. Amen.

You must be willing to risk losing what you were given, to experience success in God.

DAY 3

Position Yourself Joshua

This is the day that you will position yourself to carry out that which you have declared that which you believe to be concrete in your life. This is the day to rejoice because you have come to a place of decision with intent to cross over into your "Promises". Promises are guaranteed; however, not without opposition! This is the place to change your posture, your focus, and your usual fighting style to a radical stance. Never forget your past has been designed to challenge your future. Nonetheless, your past does not have supremacy. Use your past to tell your future "no failure and no quitting!".

Joshua 14:9 NIV *"So on that day Moses swore to me, 'The land on which your feet have walked will be your inheritance and that of your children forever, because you have followed the LORD my God wholeheartedly."*

What is your Promised Land? What book? What business? What song? What dream? What has God given you that will change your life, which in turn will give Him all the glory and bless the nation? What gift has God given you that will be a demonstration for future generations that the God you serve is more than capable of destroying your roadblocks, impossibilities, and vindicating you from appalling injustice, and then placing you in powerful positions that neither your education nor your track record has qualified you to be?

In the name of Jesus, I release unto you all my fears, my entire if's and maybe's which serve as a distraction for the plans you designed just for me. I denounce pride, and my intellectual reasoning that will attempt to orchestrate another plan for success above your plan. I accept every promise over my life; I receive it as your blessings for me. Lord Jesus, I embrace your indescribable love. "That love" searched me out to become, to lead, and be far greater than my mind ever imagined.
~I TAKE MY POSITION~

If you never begin, how will you know the outcome?

DAY 4

Be Aware of Cain

There will be days you will not feel good about walking in purpose. There will be relentless hours of trying to figure out why God has chosen you. Stop the chatter from killing your destiny. You are too close to let go of your blessings, and too close to interrupt your life through what you see and feel. Ask for wisdom to identify the assassins around you, and then ask God for the proper tools on how to use them.

Cain is waiting for an opportunity to kill your gift, your ability, your inheritance, your ministry, and your purpose. Wake up! Stand up! And move. Cain attempts to take your joy, inflict pain, as a strategy to make you forget that God loves you.

Never become so indulged in fulfilling the plan that you fail to watch, pray, and enjoy the fruit of your labor. Don't become blinded to your surroundings.

Gen. 4:3-8 NIV *"In the course of time Cain brought some of the fruits of the soil as an offering to the LORD. And Abel also brought an offering—fat portions from some of the firstborn of his flock. The LORD looked with favor on Abel and his offering, but on Cain and his offering he did not look with favor. So Cain was very angry, and his face was downcast. Then the LORD said to Cain, "Why are you angry? Why is your face downcast? If you do what is right, will you not be accepted? But if you do not do what is right, sin is crouching at your door; it desires to have you, but you must rule over it." Now Cain said to his brother Abel, "Let's go out to the field." While they were in the field, Cain attacked his brother Abel and killed him."*

In the name of Jesus, I place my entire mind, body, and soul into your hands. Father, everything within me is released unto you. Father, today I pray that when I reject the process of endurance and become frail in spirit or in liveliness, just a reminder of your love will reposition my mind and heart for your will. I decree and declare readiness, sharpness, and 20/20 spiritual vision. I decree and declare no lacking in wisdom or logic. I decree and declare no abortion to the plan. I decree and declare that all Cains are only agitators for forward movement in divine destiny.

~*I WILL NOT YIELD* ~

Your value is a gift. What will you use it for?

DAY 5

Embrace Your Process to Greater: I Am Joseph

The path that was chosen will develop you if you are willing to hold on during the process.

It's imperative that you read: Genesis chapters 37, 39, 40 and 41.
Please take the time to journey with me through Joseph's process.

Joseph's experience was necessary. When we have been chosen to become a life changer, alteration must first happen in our lives. Greater will be developed through and within your process. You will be stronger than before, acquire knowledge and wisdom for appropriate decision-making, and receive greater anointing and blessings for a successful life.

Did Joseph yield to the path that was chosen for him? "Yes". Not everyone is willing to yield to process! The formation of natural diamonds requires very high temperatures and pressures. To become, we must be able to go through. It's not a life that is glamorous. However, it's a life of denial, a life of letting go and a life of believing in God. Believing in God even when the evidence is nowhere in sight.

Transformation is necessary. You may experience the pit, prison, injustice, denial of a position, trials of all sorts, divorce, broken friendships, financial poverty, or becoming a victim at the hands of another. Don't just sit, but pour your heart out before God and seek ways to have the correct vision while looking at your situation. Your experiences will help save, change, and bring hope to those that have let go or those that have felt like no one else understood the hurt.

Has anyone ever used the term "try me?" You are in the position to try God at His word. You will be "great for the kingdom and a life changer". Give God what he's asking of you. Let God prove himself to "YOU".
Malachi 3:7-12 NIV; Psalm 34:3-8 NIV; Proverbs 3:5-6 NIV

1. Prove God to be right or wrong	2. Prove God to be a vindicator or a villain
3. Prove God to be a healer or counterfeit	4. Prove God to be a comforter or torturer
5. Prove God to be a restorer or powerless	6. Prove God to be trustworthy or unreliable

Father, I seek you today for a greater understanding of who you have been developing me to become. In the name of Jesus, would you please forgive me for becoming hostile towards you while you were stripping things away from me and for the pruning? I pour my heart out before you. I give my mind to you and my will. I come into agreement with your will over my life. I decree and declare that I will embrace and accept your nature of love. I am the trailblazer, the groundbreaker, the originator, and the dreamer that has been called to make dreams come true for others. Lord Jesus, I embrace you as absolute in my life. Amen.

~My time is now~

It was necessary.

DAY 6

Remove Me from Every Comfortable Place to An Exceptional Place

Don't leave me in this place with which I'm so comfortable. Life has seemingly had the upper hand, the final say, and even the appearance of being in control of your surroundings. "DIG DEEP" within and scream. Scream out through whatever little faith or hope you have and declare that you are still blessed, and you will keep going!

This is the time that your faith is being tested, and what you say you believe about God is on the line! Most of us learn how to adjust to a lifestyle of "just enough". Today, ask God to turn your world upside down to be shaken from the mental fatigue, the battered heart and the loss of will power to get up and move.

YOU ARE EXCEPTIONAL! Accept it. You were chosen to BE.

A good number of people, who are exceptional, whether unusually good or much better-than-average, struggle with their identity. Often, they search for relationships, friendships, careers, etc. in which they will not have to exercise their God-centered gifting or talents. Exceptional people want to excel, but only when it's related to friendships, relationships, finances, popularity, or where there is no responsibility to be a God-centered leader, or to have God-centered accountability for attachments. Exceptional people will deny who they are in order to do what they call, "being myself". They often deny the call to an extraordinary life.

Mark 14:66-72 NIV Peter denied ever knowing Jesus. Up until this point, Peter didn't have to walk in accountability for the exceptional life that God was preparing him to live. For most of us, we too want others to hold our hands through life's process to greater without counting the cost. Peter is here seen as a runner, denier, and loner. Most exceptional people will walk away from the body of Christ trying to find themselves when what they're really doing is walking directly into "life lessons", the greatest teacher of all times. After some time running and having an authentic encounter with Jesus and the Holy Spirit, Peter accepts his exceptional call of duty and changes thousands of lives. ***Acts 2:14-42 NIV***

~Life will teach you a lesson, may it be right or wrong: Life will teach you a lesson. ~

Father, I no longer use my weakness as an excuse to remain complacent or rebellious. On this day, I choose to accept and believe that I have been gifted and given great talents, strengths and abilities, and I will release myself from every place of captivity. Amen.

~I CHOOSE TO SHINE ~

Mediocre will interfere with greater.

DAY 7

I Am Who God Says I Am – I Will Accept Nothing Less than GREATER

This day, I believe in who I have been called to become. When self-doubt arises, I choose to believe and take tangible steps to continue. I will no longer be easily torn between what's right vs. what's wrong. Instead, I will embrace God's love through His instructions. When others don't believe in my change, I won't operate from a judgmental mindset. I will operate through love and from a place of understanding. After all, they have been a witness to my waywardness and my indecisiveness. I choose to walk in God's confidence, God's word, and God's promises.

The torments of my former and frustrations of my past failures must cease-and-desist from this moment! I only accept God's plan according to **Jeremiah 29:11 NIV** as my "lifeline to greatness". I embrace Jesus Christ as absolute and my foundation of faith. My belief is purely from God's Word.

~I am unlimited; I am boundless; I am abundant; I decree and declare that I am released by the blood of Jesus to become. ~

My past is only a reminder of God's grace, and God's love for my life. I declare that my destiny of "greater" will be surrounded by purposeful actions and purposeful people.

~I will walk in the apostolic call and anointing over my life ~ *Luke 4:18-19 NIV*

John 15:16 NIV *"You did not choose me, but I chose you and appointed you so that you might go and bear fruit—fruit that will last—and so that whatever you ask in my name the Father will give you."*

Allow God to become your architect and receive His blueprints as your lifeline to successful living. You are never free from challenges; however, empowered to remain, sustain, and to live out your purpose. It's time to smile. It's time to shine. Pick your head up, pick up your soul, and walk in the peace of Jesus Christ. *"NO MORE"* condemnation!

I release myself by the blood of Jesus Christ, from every soul tie, generational curse, and every voice that declared any doctrine contrary to the doctrine of Jesus Christ. I decree and declare my identity is no longer attached to anyone or anything that was not ordained by Jesus Christ. God sever, demolish, burn up any former identity look-a-likes, any former or current pretenders created by my desires, any form of emotional crises for love, affection, attention, and relational ties. I decree and declare I am free in the name of Jesus Christ.

~*I AM NOTHING LESS THAN WHOM I HAVE BEEN CALLED TO BE* ~

I don't need to be brave, just willing to accept who I was created to be.

DAY 8

I Am the Servant of the Most High God

Lord God, you know the hidden parts of my heart. Fill me with a sincere spirit, one that will dedicate itself to you through love, and not obligation. I rebuke the thoughts of serving because of necessity, guilt or because I know it's the right thing to do. God, you have anointed me to walk boldly in the prophetic realm, to prophecy, to teach, to minister the Gospel, and to compel those who have fallen, those who have given up, and those who have been tormented. I embrace serving through the guidance of the Holy Spirit, so that others may experience the joy of being healed and set free.

God, I embrace serving for the greater good of others. Father, I declare that because of my freedom, the price you paid for me, the love you continually extended to me, I will give to others through your guidance and not through my way of believing or my ideology.

I am a servant of the kingdom of God and not the world system. I will not disregard the laws and codes of the land. However, I will walk in fulfillment of them. I will use every tool from both realms to help push others beyond barriers, roadblocks, and dilemmas, be they emotional, financial or generational.

Now, I commit to a life of praying and fasting. I totally give myself over to you, without fear. I free fall into your arms, without looking back or wishing and wondering if my life could have been better or different without serving you.

Psalm 116:16 NIV "Truly I am your servant, LORD; I serve you just as my mother did; you have freed me from my chains."

Titus 1:1-3 NIV "Paul, a servant of God and an apostle of Jesus Christ to further the faith of God's elect and their knowledge of the truth that *leads to godliness-in the hope of eternal life, which God, who does not lie, promised before the beginning of time, and which now at his appointed season he has brought to light through the preaching entrusted to me by the command of God our Savior."*

Lord, I am embracing simplicity and I will enjoy life moving forward into my purpose. I will laugh; I will enjoy being a servant; and I will enjoy the divine connections you have given me, the divine friendships, family, fellow layman in the gospel, and colleagues. I will walk a balanced life, one that is free to love and laugh while at the same time knowing I can remove every layer of myself to remain rooted and grounded.

~I am your servant~

~ I am here to serve~

~ I will worship you~

The transforming power of Jesus Christ is on display in the lives of those, who have traded selfishness for selflessness.

DAY 9

An Untested Faith Will Never Excel You

Everything you have declared will be tested. Never fall into the trap of thinking because you have chosen purpose, you will never have another day's trouble, road blocks, or dead-end streets. You will. Before, you turned to habits, people, or just omitted dealing with issues all together for the sake of time and frustration. Now, you have not only been empowered, but you have access to the throne of Grace and Mercy. God will provide you every tool and resource needed for victory.

Tested faith brings experience. You could not have come to the right understanding about your imperfections if you had not been forced to pass through the rivers, and you would never have known God's strength if you had not been overtaken by the tidal waves. The more faith is tested with tribulation, the greater it intensifies in humility, love, wisdom, and power. Faith and trials are ingredients within the recipes for "A Greater YOU".

If those professing to be Christians will admit to this truth, they would testify that testing was necessary, but never welcomed. Knowing something must happen to further develop us is the very thing we dread. If I could grow without the anticipated trials, how far would I rise? If testing is necessary, then it must mean that growth is imperative!

Untested means: uncertain, untried, unapproved, unverified, uncertified, and unconfirmed. In life you must ask yourself, "Without the testing, will this conduct appropriately represent Godly character?" Allow yourself to be tested. Jesus Christ is waiting for the opportunity to be displayed within your character.

Deny running away from challenges. Deny circumventing difficult places in your path. Seek God's perfect plan for greater glory in your life.

Revelation 2:10 NIV *"Do not be afraid of what you are about to suffer. I tell you, the devil will put some of you in prison to test you, and you will suffer persecution for ten days. Be faithful, even to the point of death, and I will give you life as your victor's crown."*

Father, today I rise. I stand up, and I accept those things known and unknown that will bring superiority to my life. I call on you alone for strength to endure, faith to proceed, and a greater understanding concerning your love for me. I embrace a change of mind. I open my heart to your process for real faith. The faith in which Jesus remained on the cross even though He couldn't see you, even though He couldn't feel you, and at one point He felt the pain of being forsaken. He didn't stop the process. Lord, I want that faith. I decree and declare that same enduring power! Amen.

~Your test is necessary for your next level~

Don't panic! Embrace God's Word in this.

DAY 10

No More Training Wheels

Training wheels are needed when a child is first learning how to ride a bicycle. Over a period as the child grows, those training wheels must be removed. Two important lessons must be acquired during this process.

First: Listening must take place. When I was learning how to ride my bicycle with the training wheels, it was fun and I spent countless hours some days riding. As time passed, my father sat with me, explaining why the training wheels had to be removed. He said, "Lynn, you will fall, it may hurt but continue to get up again." As a child would be, I was excited for something different. It became difficult very quickly listening to my father's voice, unlike previously. I began experiencing pain from falling repeatedly. I remember throwing the bike down, as if the bike was the object of my pain, to somehow prove that I didn't need it any longer and I wasn't going to ride it again. Eventually, I listened to my father; I learned to ride my bicycle without training wheels.

In this Christian walk, as believers we do that as well. We withdraw from the word of God when we are experiencing growing pains. We have the tendency to cease from praying as if prayer is the object of our growing pains! We blame God for the turbulence and stop following Him altogether.

Second: Following instructions must take place.

Never allow life experiences to lead you away from the instructions of the Word. We all need these experiences like the removal of the training wheels. Never allow your achievements to drive you into making a common mistake believers make: over-confidence and self-righteousness.

- Believers must continue following and listening for guidance through the Holy Spirit. As a believer grows through experiences, keep an open heart for God's love and a willingness to receive His instructions for continued growth and development.
- I will not allow myself to become self-governed. I will use my training to increase in spiritual wisdom so that I can make applicable assessments in life situations with correct understanding.

Ephesians 4:14-16 NIV *"Then we will no longer be infants, tossed back and forth by the waves, and blown here and there by every wind of teaching and by the cunning and craftiness of people in their deceitful scheming. Instead, speaking the truth in love, we will grow to become in every respect the mature body of him who is the head, that is, Christ. From him the whole body, joined and held together by every supporting ligament, grows and builds itself up in love, as each part does its work."*

In the name of Jesus, I release myself from every pity party, every place of immaturity, known and unknown to me. I am responsible, and I will hold myself accountable, In the name of Jesus Christ. Amen.

~I need to grow, or I will become spiritually impaired~

You are never alone.

DAY 11

The Rain Must Fall

The mandate demands blessings upon my life. The shower of God's love, His forgiveness, His peace is upon my life. I am blessed with abundance and favor. I am released to become greater than my past struggles, my past sins, and the sins of my forefathers.

God's rain is my sanctuary, my time of refreshing, my time of peaceful thinking and flowing in His genuine love for me! I feel the rain. I feel the peace of God all over me. I can laugh now. I can enjoy life now. No more self-inflicted dreary days; no more self-inflicted breakdowns or break ups. Those days are over.

Job 9:27 NIV *"If I say, 'I will forget my complaint, I will change my expression, and smile,'"*

Today, I walk and live under His showers of blessings. I will dance to the sound of the rain. God's drops are renewed strength to my soul. I am healed within my inner parts. My soul rejoices over His love to heal my deepest hurts, my secrets, and those unimaginable things I kept within my heart. I am blessed to have open access to Jesus and His sovereign love.

Psalm 96:1-5 NIV *"Sing to the Lord a new song; sing to the Lord, all the earth. Sing to the Lord, praise his name; proclaim his salvation day after day. Declare his glory among the nations, his marvelous deeds among all peoples. For great is the Lord and most worthy of praise; he is to be feared above all gods. For all the gods of the nations are idols, but the Lord made the heavens."*

I decree and declare; my worship will reflect a renewed relationship in Jesus Christ. My praises will be an echo to the ears of God's people with a viewpoint of redemption. I feel the rain; it showers me with God's love for me. I am worthy to be called His very own, no more condemnation from a self-inflicted and tormented mind.

I remove the rain boots that have served as a defense mechanism from walking out the plan that you have over my life. I walk bare footed before you so that my steps are divinely orchestrated by your will. I remove my raincoat that has served as a wall, which has hindered divine growth and development; and receiving your love in abundance. Lord, I want to be drenched holistically. I get rid of my rain cap which represents my analytical and tactical reasoning against truth, against those things which I know have been designed for a successful life in you. I feel the rain against my subconscious and my deepest known and unknown thoughts.

~I refuse to walk in cover-ups & defenses that will sabotage my destiny~

~Let the rain fall; I walk and play in the raindrops of God's love~

Grow more and more into the image of God's Love.

DAY 12

God Loves Me and I Accept His Forgiveness Over My Life

Today, I accept God's love over my life, and the weight of my sins will no longer cause me to imprison myself, exhaust myself, rest in guilt, or succumb to a pity party. I will not dwell on all the dreadful things that I've done against God.

Today, I am willing to face the consequences of my sins without condemnation. I choose to accept God's grace and mercy. I believe in Jesus' redeeming power from all bondages, from self-hatred, self-injury, depression and all known and unknown habits that influenced my performance, my attitude, conduct and character.

I will walk in truth. I refuse to cover up. I refuse to justify myself with a non-caring attitude towards those that I injured along the way, the relationships that were severed and damaged to protect my feelings and my reputation.

God, the Father, will not hear your prayers if you are holding any kind of unforgiveness towards anyone, **including yourself!!** *Mark 11:25 NIV*

Open yourself for God's love: I will love myself through the love God has released unto me. I accept nothing less from myself. I will stop weeping over my mistakes; I will discontinue dreading to cross paths with my past and become prepared to handle it according to God's will.

I am-Free: ***Romans 8:1-2 NIV***

I am-Healed: ***Jeremiah 30:17 NIV; Psalm 147:3 NIV; Luke 4:14, 18 NIV***

I am-Released: ***John 8:36 NIV; 2 Corinthians 3:17 NIV***

Today is the best day of my life! I believe in freedom, in His grace and mercy. His sovereign love is displayed through Him being a God of "another chance" and a God of redemption. Today, He has given me victory that I didn't deserve and a love I was unworthy of.

Psalm 32:2 NIV *"Blessed is the one whose sin the Lord does not count against them and in whose spirit is no deceit."*

Father, in the name of Jesus, I am free to love myself. I am free to accept your grace and mercy. I believe in your love. I believe my life is worth receiving your love. I denounce every false statement that I made against my destiny. I decree and declare that my past no longer has control over me. I am no longer in agreement with my past. I forgive myself and I let go of trying to prove my change.

~I believe that I am forgiven~

What will you believe?

DAY 13

Purpose Is My Purpose

This is where you will understand your purpose, thereby becoming the mirror, the image of Jesus Christ. You are more than just your works in the Kingdom. If that was your thinking, you will be enlightened. According to **2 Corinthians 5:20 NIV** You are an Ambassador for Christ. An ambassador is an authorized messenger or representative; a diplomat of the highest rank, accredited as representative.

I yield to whom I am to be. I will represent the King with integrity, dignity, and honor. I believe in my purpose. His aim will lead me into victorious places; I strive for "Greater". I will represent Jesus with conviction and faith. As I progress and achieve in purpose, I will never forget God's love and kindness in my life. I move without limitations. I have been endorsed as a child of the "Most High God".

"You have a divine Purpose. God has designed you to achieve it. Purpose is the object toward which one strives or for which something exists; an aim".

Isaiah 46:10 NIV *"I make known the end from the beginning, from ancient times, what is still to come. I say, 'My purpose will stand, and I will do all that I please.'"*

Proverbs 19:21 NIV *"Many are the plans in a person's heart, but it is the Lord's purpose that prevails."*

I declare that my life was reconciled by Jesus Christ. He sacrificed himself to save me, and I will carry out the exact purpose which is the "ministry of reconciliation".

Lord, I give you me! My aim will be to represent you in every aspect of my life, as a spouse, as a friend, as a son or daughter, co-worker, and a Minister of the gospel. I refuse to aim for anything less than my purpose. Lord, I know that all the treasures of this earth are yours and with you; therefore, they are mine! I don't have to compromise to attain them.

Purpose will only be satisfying when it's embraced. Without embracing, a continual fight will exist and the very thing that was implemented for my success, peace and joy will cease. My purpose is my lifeline.

I decree and declare upon my life that I will not lose sight of purpose; neither will the vision of the end goal be abandoned. I decree and declare the plans of God, favor, influence, and jurisdiction in the territory that has been given to me to accomplish divine destiny. Lord, you touched and shifted the 12 disciples. In turn, they changed the nation concerning who you are. That initial act from you released "Greatness upon this earth" and upon mankind. As did the old great leaders, I hunger to be an agent of change, a legendary model of purpose. I am willing to embark into Greater. Amen

~*I choose to Worship*~

Don't be afraid to invest in your purpose.

DAY 14

I Will Never Be the Same

Speak up Peter, speak up Paul. Transformation was required, stripping was required, and testing was required to proceed into Greater! Your name may not change, however, your character, conduct, faith, anointing, gifting and your talents will never be the same. Higher and deeper your roots of faith are, so shall you.

Lives are now being shifted. Families, colleagues, peers, and friendships will never be the same. Through the shaking, the testing, the trying of your character and conduct that took place in plain sight, it was necessary for the witnesses.

What denotes change? When control is relinquished and embracing completely to live out God's purpose in your life.

My encounter with God's love has invigorated my heart, mind, and soul. His love has spoken very clearly.

My encounter with purpose has changed my attitude.

Two important things are transparency to God and allowing the Holy Spirit to lead.

Peter returned from a place of bitterness only to walk into a place of reconciliation. He became a world-renowned life shifter, teacher, apostle, and evangelist. Paul returned from a place of judgment, to know God on a level that caused an astronomical change in the spiritual realm and social economics.

The Apostle Paul in **Acts 9:1-31 NIV,** isn't the same person in **Acts 7:58 NIV**; he was a by stander in Stephen's death, and a persecutor of the Christians in **Acts 8 NIV** and **9:1-2 NIV**. The Apostle Peter in **Acts 2 and 3**

NIV isn't the same person in **Matthew 26:31-75 NIV**. There are many examples of authentic transformation. Begin your new life and journey in the identity for which you were created to be.

Father, I decree and declare I will be led by the Holy Spirit. I decree and declare authentic evidence will be shown, according to **Galatians 5:22-23; 25 NIV** *"But the fruit of the Spirit is love, joy, peace, patience, kindness, goodness, faithfulness, gentleness, and self-control. Against such things there is no law. 25 "Since we live by the Spirit, let us keep in step with the Spirit."*

In the name of Jesus Christ, I embrace your will, plans and instructions over my life. Lord, when I grow weary, weak and fearful, I choose to take responsibility of trusting you. Lord, this one thing I do know, in all my imperfections, "your strength, power and love are enough to keep me". Since I am directed by your word to live by the Spirit, let me keep in step with the Spirit in all my ways.

~It's time to enjoy the freedom of love and reconciliation. ~

~I AM NO LONGER THE SAME~

My destiny is my lifeline.

Apostle Melinda J. Sutton is the Founder of Divine Glory Ministries, Inc. She is the wife of Chief Apostle Jesse Sutton, a mother, and grandmother. Melinda's desire is solely to love God, serve his people, and change lives through the Gospel. She has experienced many life altering circumstances including receiving a medical prognosis and ministry partners walking away from their assignment. Yet, she allowed her fears and disappointments to face the Word of God. Her heart's cry has been "I just want to do ministry". Anyone that has encountered her will know she genuinely loves people, she will give her last to others in need, and she will preach the uncompromised gospel unapologetically.

Apostle Melinda J. Sutton was raised in Malone, Florida where she learned the fundamentals of Christianity. Years later, she moved to Bradenton, Florida and joined Bethlehem Baptist Church in Sarasota under the leadership of Rev. Patrick A. Miller, who became her spiritual father. While there, Melinda served in many auxiliaries and was prepared for a greater work to minister the Gospel. It was there that she became intimately acquainted with the struggle of people of different backgrounds to believe God's word.

In 2005, God led Melinda to Tallahassee, Florida where she served as a collegiate director. In 2007, Rev. Patrick A. Miller established Melinda as the Pastor of Bethlehem Baptist Church of Tallahassee (B.B.C.T.), known today as Divine Glory Ministries, Inc. (D.G.M.). One of her greatest accomplishments is having trained a group of college students to live according to God's word in such a secular society. Many of these same students have become devoted and comprehensive believers. She has experienced the scrutiny of many leaders because of her stance, "For God I live and for God I die" and her ability to persevere in a male dominated position.

On October 18, 2020, Chief Apostle Jesse Sutton reaffirmed Apostle Melinda J. Sutton and accepted the call and responsibility of being Overseer of Divine Glory Ministries, Inc.

In November of 2020, she married Chief Apostle Jesse Sutton, "Her King". She continues to Pastor Divine Glory Ministries, Inc. while raising up qualified believers to lead the people of God. In addition, she is the Vice Presider of Global Enrichment Ministries, Uniting the Kingdom International Ministries, and Global Regional Conference Coordinators, alongside her husband.

Melinda is the author of "The Power of Prayer: Believing for a Transformed Life" and "From Him, Through Me, To You". With more literary works on the horizon, she is allowing her gift to reach many nations and aspires to preach the gospel to all ends of the Earth.

Made in the USA
Columbia, SC
28 October 2023